11.40

DATE DUE

AUG 2 3 1995

DATE DUE

© Aladdin Books Ltd 1988

Designed and produced by
Aladdin Books Ltd
70 Old Compton Street
London W1

Design   David West
Children's Book Design
Editorial Planning   Clark Robinson Limited
Editor   Bibby Whittaker
Researcher   Cecilia Weston-Baker
Illustrated by   Ron Hayward Associates

EDITORIAL PANEL
The author, Lionel Bender, is an
author, editor and producer of
children's illustrated general science
and natural history books.

The educational consultant, Peter
Thwaites, is Head of Geography at
Windlesham House School in
Sussex ,UK

The editorial consultant, John Clark,
has contributed to many
information and reference books.

First published in the
United States in 1988 by
Gloucester Press
387 Park Avenue South
New York, NY 10016

ISBN 0-531-17091-8

Library of Congress Catalog
Card Number: 87-82896

TODAY'S WORLD

BIRDS AND MAMMALS

LIONEL BENDER

GLOUCESTER PRESS
New York · London · Toronto · Sydney

CONTENTS

How the book works

Each section of the book describes a group of related animals. Each begins with an introduction and a large diagram of a typical animal from the group. Smaller diagrams explain the heart and blood circulation, and the structure of the animal's skeleton. Other pages have diagrams and color photographs that illustrate important points discussed in the text. Throughout the book, charts provide a comparison of the forms and sizes of representative animals in a particular group. All illustrations are drawn to scale.

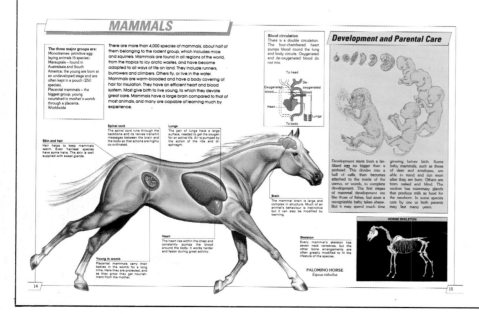

The cover photograph shows a cheetah with her cub.

INTRODUCTION

Birds were the first warm-blooded animals to take to the air. They have evolved into a wide variety of forms to take advantage of all habitats on Earth, and all kinds of foods. Some specialize in eating plant foods – fruit, nuts, seeds and even honey and nectar. Others have a diet consisting entirely of insects. And yet others are efficient hunters, feeding on other animals, including snakes and fish. From the Arctic to the tropics, on land and in the water, every region of the world has its bird life. But all share the common feature of laying eggs.

Apart from one or two primitive species, all mammals give birth to live young, which initially feed on mother's milk. They share a basic four-legged body plan, although in some – such as seals and whales – the limbs have become flippers for swimming and they share their habitats with fish. In bats, the front limbs have evolved as wings so that they can fly and compete with birds. And as with birds, mammals include plant-eaters, insect-eaters and meat-eaters, which among them populate every region on Earth.

A group of hippopotamuses wallow in a weed-covered river in Zambia.

BIRDS

There are 27 groups of birds.
Biggest group: Passerines, the perching birds. This includes familiar types such as crows and sparrows (5,150 species).
Smallest group: Struthioniformes, with just one species, the ostrich.
Most common species: African quelea finch – more than 100 billion.
Rarest species: California condor – fewer than 10 in the wild.

There are about 8,500 different species or kinds of birds, making them the most numerous backboned animals living on land. They range in size from tiny hummingbirds only 5.5cm (2.2in) long to the ostrich, which may be more than 2.2m (7ft) tall. They are found on every continent and in all habitats from tropical forest and desert to arctic tundra and ice. But they all have in common the fact that they are warm-blooded – that is, they can keep their bodies at a constant temperature, usually about 40°C (104°F). The front limbs – legs in most reptiles and mammals – have become modified as wings, usually used for flight, and feathers provide the main body covering, with scales on the legs and toes. Feathers trap heat under them and provide large surfaces needed for flight. Birds have no teeth, but have lightweight beaks (made of horn) covering the jaws.

Flight

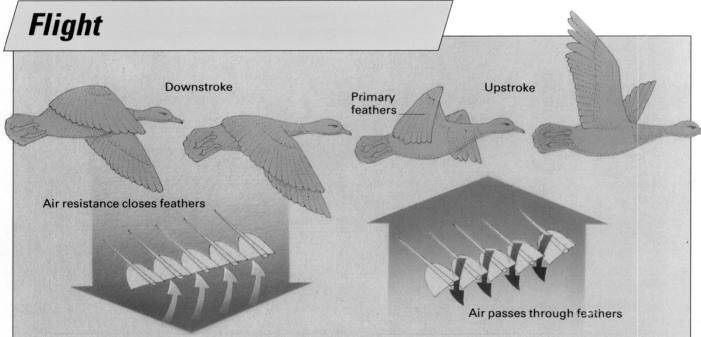

Downstroke

Primary feathers

Upstroke

Air resistance closes feathers

Air passes through feathers

The streamlined shape of a bird helps it slip easily through the air as it flies, driven through the air by its wings acting as propellers. The power to work the wings comes from large muscles on the bird's chest on each side of the breastbone. Tendons run from these to the wing bones. There is little muscle in the wings themselves, which are light and easy to swing. The inner part of the wings helps give the bird lift as it moves forward. It acts rather like the wing of an airplane. The outer part of the wings, with its long primary feathers, gives the forward push, with the primaries bending so that they help the animal forward on the upstroke as well as the downstroke. As the bird makes a downstroke the feathers are flattened against the air, making an airtight surface. On the upstroke they are turned so that air can spill between them. Flying actions and the wing shapes are adapted to the animals' needs and the type of country they inhabit.

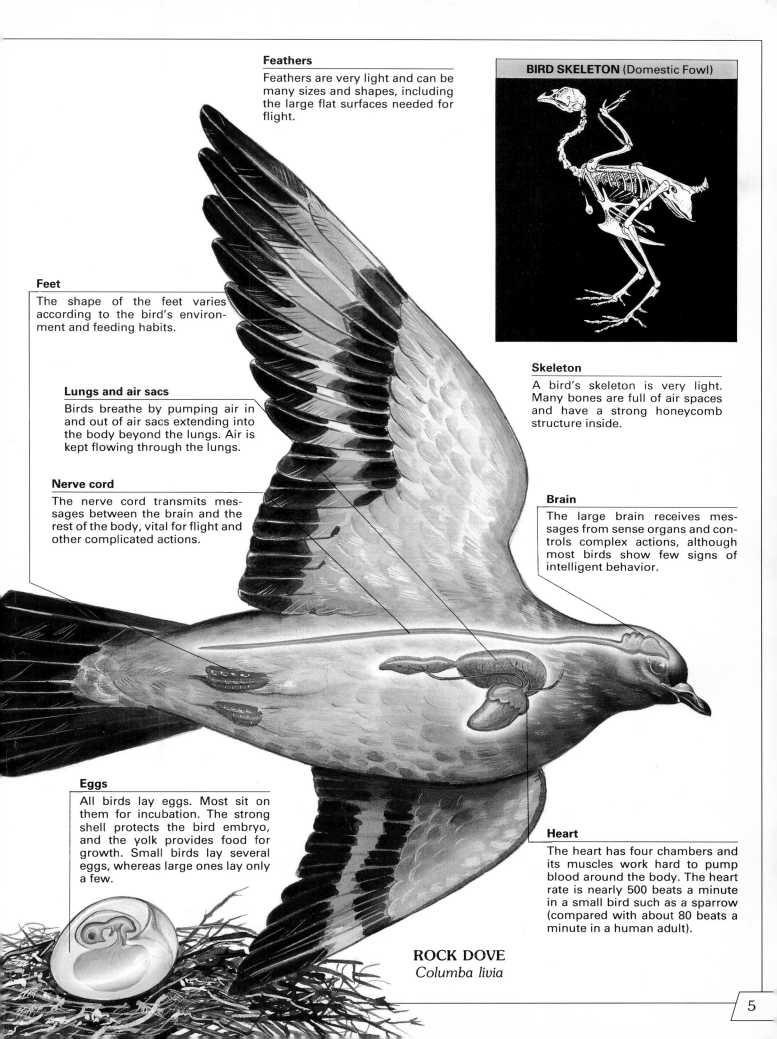

Feathers

Feathers are very light and can be many sizes and shapes, including the large flat surfaces needed for flight.

BIRD SKELETON (Domestic Fowl)

Feet

The shape of the feet varies according to the bird's environment and feeding habits.

Lungs and air sacs

Birds breathe by pumping air in and out of air sacs extending into the body beyond the lungs. Air is kept flowing through the lungs.

Nerve cord

The nerve cord transmits messages between the brain and the rest of the body, vital for flight and other complicated actions.

Skeleton

A bird's skeleton is very light. Many bones are full of air spaces and have a strong honeycomb structure inside.

Brain

The large brain receives messages from sense organs and controls complex actions, although most birds show few signs of intelligent behavior.

Eggs

All birds lay eggs. Most sit on them for incubation. The strong shell protects the bird embryo, and the yolk provides food for growth. Small birds lay several eggs, whereas large ones lay only a few.

Heart

The heart has four chambers and its muscles work hard to pump blood around the body. The heart rate is nearly 500 beats a minute in a small bird such as a sparrow (compared with about 80 beats a minute in a human adult).

ROCK DOVE
Columba livia

SEED- AND INSECT-EATERS

Major types: Seed-eaters include pigeons, parrots and specialist feeders such as finches. Other birds, ranging from ostriches to pheasants, take seeds as part of their diet. Insect-eaters include specialist types such as swifts, bee-eaters and treecreepers. Plant-eating birds often feed their young on insects.

Seeds and insects are two of the most abundant sources of food for birds, and there are more birds specialized for these diets than for any other. Insects may be caught in the air by swallows and nightjars, picked from the surface of leaves and twigs by warblers, dug out from bark by woodpeckers, or scratched from the soil. Seeds can also be gathered in many ways, but they are harder to digest. Seed-eating birds have strong muscular gizzards, or grinding-stomachs, in which seeds are ground by the grit swallowed with the food. The first part of the gut, the crop, stores food after it is swallowed. The food is ground by the grit in the gizzard and digested.

Beaks and food

Some birds have all-purpose beaks and feed on many foods. Specialists feed on just one type of food and usually have a beak that is fully adapted to make the best job of the vital task of feeding. Many seed-eaters have a short conical beak, good for picking and cracking seeds. But there are variations depending on which seeds they eat most. Among finches, the bullfinch has a large powerful bill; it feeds on seeds, buds and shoots. The redpoll uses its smaller narrower bill like tweezers for picking the small seeds of birch and other trees. The oddly shaped beak of the crossbill can extract seeds from the cones of firs and pines.

Insect-eaters tend to have rather thin pointed beaks which they use like forceps to pick at their small prey, but again there are many variations according to the insect prey and the catching method used. Birds such as swifts that chase insects in the air have a huge gape to act as an aerial fishing net. The treecreeper has a thin beak that can be pushed deep into bark crevices. The long, strong beak of a woodpecker can drill a hole in bark so the long tongue can be used to probe for insects underneath. The Hawaiian akiapolaau also probes bark for insects with its long beak, whereas the Maui parrotbill tears into bark with its powerful beak to reach beetles.

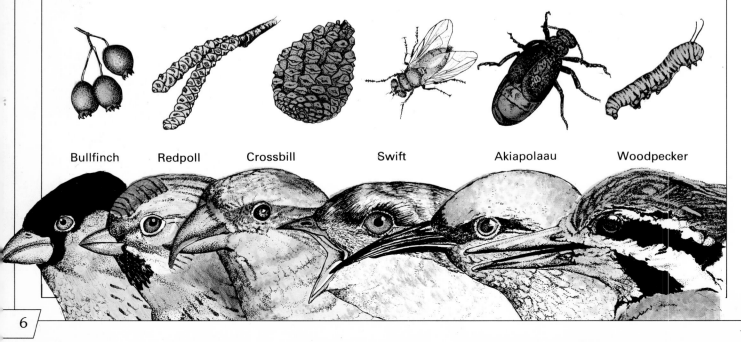

Bullfinch   Redpoll   Crossbill   Swift   Akiapolaau   Woodpecker

Care of plumage

A bird must keep its feathers in good condition if they are to function properly. A small bird may have as many as 3,000 feathers, a big bird more than 20,000. Birds molt or shed old feathers, with new ones growing below at regular intervals. The feathers are lost in a regular sequence, a few at a time, equally balanced on each side of the body. They are kept in condition by frequent preening, when the bird uses its beak and claws to tidy and comb them. It smears the feathers with a thin layer of waterproofing oil from a preen gland at the base of the tail. Many birds take baths in shallow pools, dipping and shaking their plumage. These actions discourage parasites such as mites and lice.

A small bird washing its feathers

Nests

The chicks of most small seed-eaters and insect-eaters are hatched naked and helpless, and are fed by their parents for many days before they are able to look after themselves. As adults, these birds build nests in which to lay their eggs and rear their families. Some, like chickadees, nest in tree holes, lining the cavity. Many make cup nests in trees and bushes, using a variety of materials. The reed warbler, for example, weaves a nest of grass. The most elaborately woven nests are those of weaver birds, which often make their ball nests in colonies. Many martins make cup nests and South American ovenbirds make large enclosed nests using plastered mud and blades of grass.

A woodpecker makes a hole in a tree for a nest.

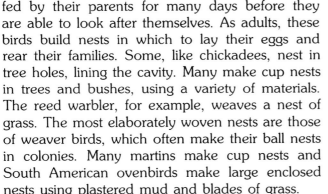

Reed warbler

Weaver bird

Sand martin

Ovenbird

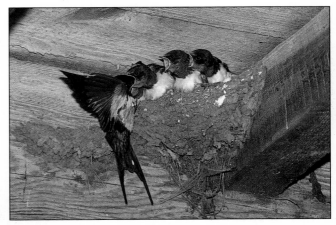

Swallows make nests of mud.

BIRDS OF PREY

Diurnal or daytime types:
Order Falconiformes – about 280 species, including falcons, eagles, hawks and vultures.
Largest: Andean condor – 1.15m (3.7ft) long. **Smallest:** Pygmy falcon – 14cm (5.5in) long. **Nocturnal or nighttime types:** Order Strigiformes, the owls (over 130 species).
Largest: Great eagle owl – 60cm (2ft) long. **Smallest:** Elf owl – 13cm (5in) long.

Birds of prey are adapted to eating other animals. Some are effective hunters, with beaks and claws to kill and tear large prey apart. Others, including many of the largest vultures, are scavengers feeding on the bodies of dead animals. A few feed on insects, snails or fish. Most birds of prey are expert fliers. Some pursue prey at high speed, others are best suited for soaring, sailing through the sky for long periods before homing in on prey or carrion. But many spend much of their life at rest. Their food is nourishing and they do not need frequent meals. If they can hunt efficiently when required, they can also relax when they are not hungry.

Feeding

An osprey is a hawk that catches fish.

Owls, eagles, falcons and hawks kill their prey by grasping with their powerful talons (toes and claws). Their beaks are also powerful, with hooked tips, but are usually reserved for pulling the food apart once it is caught. Vultures feed on carrion and do not need strong claws, but their beaks are strong for tearing flesh. Owls generally swallow prey whole, whereas others tear food into small pieces. The size and type of feet are closely linked to the food the birds eat. An osprey feeds on fish and has sharp scales beneath the toes to hold slippery prey. It has two toes pointing forward and two back. Owls can reverse one toe, but most other birds of prey have three forward toes and one back.

Vultures feeding on the remains of a zebra

Hawk beak

Falcon talon

Flying

Owls have feathers with fringes that make their flight almost silent. Many hunt by sound and their prey also hears well, so silent attack is a big advantage. Some birds of prey rely on speed of flight to catch prey. A peregrine can dive at 320 km/h (200mph). At the other extreme the kestrel can hover over a spot, searching the ground below for possible prey before dropping on it. Short, broad wings allow maneuverability in woods, while long, thin wings permit speed in open country.

A female kestrel hovers, looking for prey.

Senses

Birds of prey have forward-facing eyes that help them to judge distances as they strike at prey. Daytime hunters have very sharp vision, and some may be able to see objects six times smaller or further away than we can. Owls' enormous eyes can see in very dim light. They also have large sensitive ears, which often are a different size on each side of the head. Some pinpoint prey accurately by sound alone. Birds generally have little sense of smell, but vultures can smell carrion from a distance.

An owl has large eyes to see at night.

Hatching

Compared to other birds, some birds of prey lay few eggs. Some of the large eagles lay only one or two eggs in a clutch, and may not lay every year. The incubation period is also long, sometimes a month or more. When the chick is ready to hatch it breaks through the shell using the egg-tooth on the end of its beak. However, the chick still faces a long period of dependence on its parents. A hen bird usually lays her eggs at intervals of a day or so. Many species begin to incubate only when the complete clutch is laid. But birds of prey often incubate from the time the first egg is laid. Thus if there are several eggs, the babies also hatch at intervals. The difference in age is apparent through the nest life, and the oldest and strongest are most likely to survive. A nest of owls may contain youngsters in several stages of plumage growth.

A short-toed eagle hatching from its egg

Major types: Grebes and loons (25 species) swim and dive well. Albatrosses and petrels (90) are oceanic birds. Pelicans, cormorants and relatives (57) fish well. Ducks and geese (150) are mostly freshwater species, gulls and auks (117) seawater. Waders (213) and storks, flamingoes, cranes and rails (197) frequent a variety of habitats.

Many birds make their living in or beside water. There is scarcely a watery habitat, whether it is swamp, lake, river or sea, which is not inhabited by birds. Some, like waders, take their food from the edge of the water or from where the shore is exposed by the tide. Others, such as albatrosses, petrels and auks, spend nearly all their lives at sea, coming to land only to nest. Many waterbirds swim well, propelling themselves with their feet. Others, for instance auks and penguins, use their wings to row underwater. Those that concentrate on diving into the water to feed have well-waterproofed plumage and denser bones than other birds to help them penetrate the water.

Feeding

Waterbirds feed on many different types of food. Several, such as swans and numerous ducks, are vegetarian. They reach below the surface with their beaks for water plants. There are many fish-eaters, often with long pointed beaks to seize prey. Some of them have adaptations to hold slippery prey. For example, the cormorant has a beak with a hooked tip, and the pochard has a beak with a toothed edge. Only one type of bird, the darter, uses its sharp beak as a spear to catch fish. Pelicans, too, have a unique way of scooping up fish, using the big pouch on the lower beak as a fishing net. They sometimes work in groups to round up a shoal of fish. Most fish-eaters swallow prey whole, head first. Flamingoes feed on microscopic plants and animals. They have a sieve-like beak to extract food from the water. They wade in the shallows and dip their head in upside down. Some ducks also sieve for small organisms. Herons also wade, but stalk and wait for larger prey such as fish and frogs, as do some storks. Along the edges of both fresh and sea water, waders such as sandpipers, curlews, plovers and avocets search for food. Some pick up shellfish. Others probe mud at various depths for worms. A few dabble in water for small animals. Among waterbirds competition for food is rarely serious.

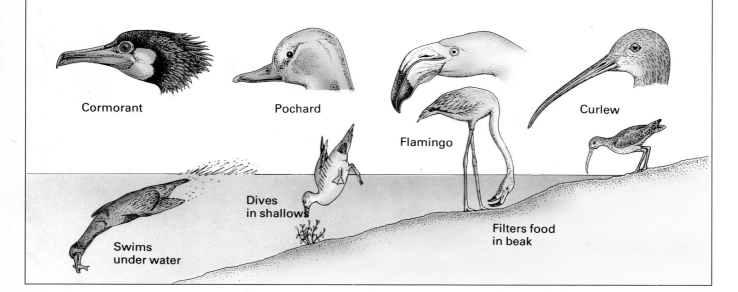

Cormorant

Pochard

Flamingo

Curlew

Swims under water

Dives in shallows

Filters food in beak

Feet

Many birds that wade need to spread their weight to save themselves from sinking into soft mud. They can do this by having long toes or webbing between the toes. The jacana, which walks over lily pads on the surface, has the longest toes of all. A common adaptation among waterbirds that are good swimmers is to have the front three toes joined by webbing, as in ducks and gulls. This provides a large surface with which to push against the water. Cormorants, shags and their relatives have all four toes joined by webbing. Some birds have lobes on their toes instead of a full web. These include the grebes and coots. Birds that propel themselves under water with their wings use webbed feet as rudders.

Great crested grebe
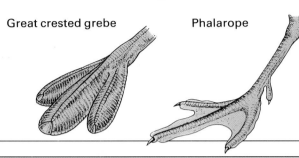

Phalarope
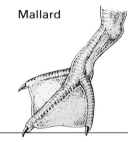

Mallard

Shag
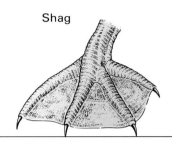

Nests

Waterbirds nest in a variety of ways. Some, such as herons, make a nest of sticks in a tree. Others stay close to the water and make a pile of vegetation to serve as a nest. In species such as coots and grebes, this nest may actually be floating. Many waders and gulls make nests that are little more than a scrape on the ground or a depression in sand or pebbles. Both eggs and young of these birds may be camouflaged. Some seabirds simply lay eggs on a cliff ledge. These eggs are pointed at one end, so they do not easily roll off.

Puffins nest in crevices on cliff tops.

Mating

Even in the most crowded seabird colonies, parents attend their own chicks and no others. A male and female must recognize one another, stay faithful, and care for their young for the population to survive. In some long-lived birds such as albatrosses, pairs often mate together for life. Outside the breeding season the parents may live apart. Many oceanic species spend most of the year scattered far from land but gather in colonies at favored sites for breeding. Sometimes thousands of birds take over a rocky island.

Courtship display of blue-footed boobies

FLIGHTLESS BIRDS

Major types: Big, running birds – ostrich (1 species), rheas (2), cassowaries (3), emu (1).
Large-bodied, short-legged, nocturnal species – kiwis (3).
Expert swimmers and divers – penguins (16).
Oddities – island rails (about 10).

Considering the advantages of flight, a surprising number of birds are flightless. Often these live in places where there are few enemies on land. On islands dotted around the world are species, closely related to birds that normally fly well, which have lost the power of flight. Then there are species adapted to running, such as rheas and emus. These are so large and swift on foot that they can outrun their enemies. They show some features of the flightless ancestors of modern birds (which evolved from reptiles), such as loose feathers and lack of a large, keeled breastbone. Scientists argue whether in evolution these birds lost the power of flight or whether they ever had it.

Movement

The large running birds have long legs with powerful thigh muscles. They do not perch so have no need of a back toe on the foot, and this has been lost, leaving three front toes. The ostrich has lost another toe, leaving one hoof-like toe and a smaller side one. An ostrich can run at 65 km/h (40mph). When running it may hold its wings out to help it balance. Although penguins cannot take to the air, their wings are not useless. They have evolved as compact paddles used to 'fly' through the water. Penguins are fast in pursuit of prey – some travel so fast in water they can shoot straight out on to a rock high above the sea. Their legs are set far back and are used as rudders.

Incubating

Some of the flightless birds look after their eggs in unusual ways. Male ostriches may mate with several females, which may all lay eggs in one nest. The male takes a large share of incubation. In emus, rheas and cassowaries, it is just the male that incubates the eggs and looks after the young. Some penguins make a nest; others lay single eggs that are held on the feet to incubate.

An ostrich can run quickly.

A penguin dives for fish.

Cassowary incubating eggs

Bird chart

Mostly meat-eating birds

Mostly plant-eating birds

Sulphur-breasted toucan
Ramphastos sulfuratus
S. America, tropical
forest

Brown pelican
Pelecanus occidentalis
N. and S. America,
coastal waters

Canada goose
Branta canadensis
N. America, wetlands

Belted kingfisher
Ceryle alcyon
N. and S. America, near
water

Whooping crane
Grus americana
N. America, swamps.
Rare

Scarlet macaw
Ara macao
S. America, tropical
forest

Mallard
Anas platyrhynchos
Worldwide, mainly
freshwater

Greater flamingo
Phoenicopterus ruber
Americas, Eurasia, Africa,
lakes, lagoons, shores

Bald eagle
Haliaeetus leucocephalus
N. America, near water

Osprey
Pandion haliaetus
Worldwide, near water

Ring-necked pheasant
Phasianus colchicus
Asia, introduced
elsewhere, woodland

King penguin
Aptenodytes patagonica
Cold southern seas

Frigate bird
Fregata magnificens
Tropical oceans

**Crimson topaz
hummingbird**
Topaza pella
S. America, tropical
forest

Peregrine falcon
Falco peregrinus
Worldwide, open country

Wandering albatross
Diomedia exulans
Southern oceans

Barn swallow
Hirundo rustica
Worldwide, open country

Andean condor
Vultur gryphus
S. America, mountains
and cliffs

Barn owl
Tyto alba
Worldwide, open country

**Red-plumed bird of
paradise**
Paradisaea apoda
New Guinea, tropical
forest

Each side of a square represents 150mm (6 inches)

13

MAMMALS

The three major groups are:
Monotremes- primitive egg-laying animals (3 species).
Marsupials – found in Australasia and South America; the young are born at an undeveloped stage and are often kept in a pouch (266 species).
Placental mammals – the biggest group; young nourished in mother's womb through a placenta. Worldwide.

There are more than 4,000 species of mammals, about half of them belonging to the rodent group, which includes mice and squirrels. Mammals are found in all regions of the world, from the tropics to icy arctic wastes, and have become adapted to all ways of life on land. They include runners, burrowers and climbers. Others fly, or live in the water. Mammals are warm-blooded and have a body covering of hair for insulation. They have an efficient heart and blood system. Most give birth to live young, to which they devote great care. Mammals have a large brain compared to that of most animals, and many are capable of learning much by experience.

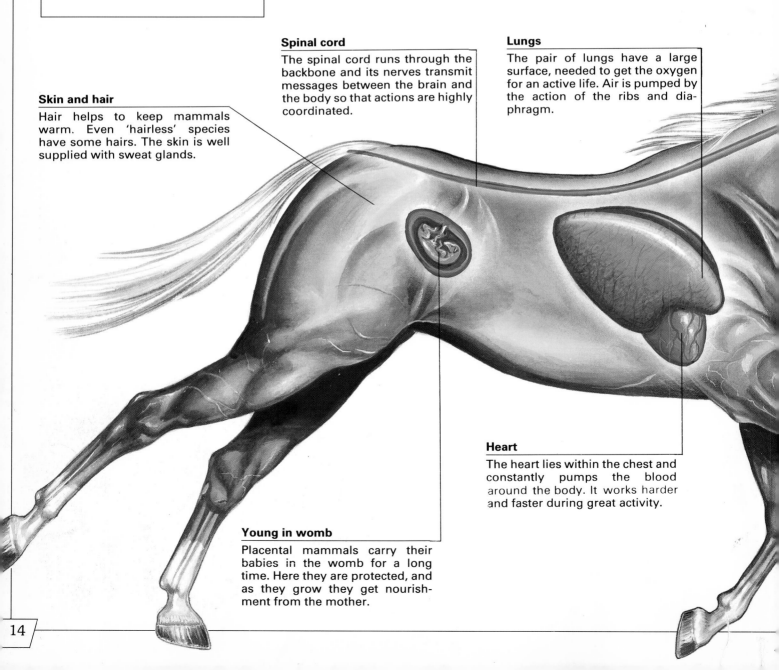

Spinal cord
The spinal cord runs through the backbone and its nerves transmit messages between the brain and the body so that actions are highly coordinated.

Lungs
The pair of lungs have a large surface, needed to get the oxygen for an active life. Air is pumped by the action of the ribs and diaphragm.

Skin and hair
Hair helps to keep mammals warm. Even 'hairless' species have some hairs. The skin is well supplied with sweat glands.

Heart
The heart lies within the chest and constantly pumps the blood around the body. It works harder and faster during great activity.

Young in womb
Placental mammals carry their babies in the womb for a long time. Here they are protected, and as they grow they get nourishment from the mother.

Blood circulation

There is a double circulation. The four-chambered heart pumps blood through the lung and body circuits. Oxygenated (red) and deoxygenated (blue) blood do not mix.

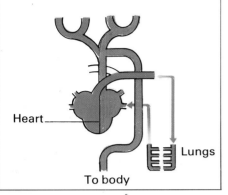

To head

Heart

Lungs

To body

Development and Parental Care

Development starts from a fertilized egg no bigger than a pinhead. This divides into a ball of cells, then becomes attached to the inside of the uterus, or womb, to complete development. The first stages of mammal development are like those of fish, but soon a recognizable baby takes shape. It may then spend much time growing before birth. Some baby mammals, such as those of deer and antelopes, are able to stand and run soon after they are born. Others are born naked and blind. The mother has mammary glands that produce milk as food for the newborn. In some species care by one or both parents may last many years.

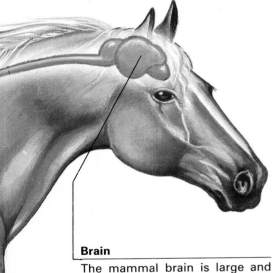

Brain

The mammal brain is large and complex in structure. Much of a mammal's behavior is instinctive but it can also be modified by learning.

Skeleton

Every mammal's skeleton has seven neck vertebrae, but the other bone arrangements are often greatly modified to fit the lifestyle of the species.

PALOMINO HORSE
Equus caballus

HORSE SKELETON

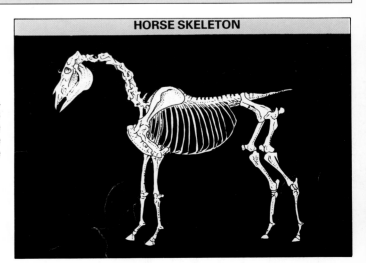

15

The Mammal World

Present-day land mammals of the world are often divided into groups representing six major geographical regions – the Nearctic, Neotropical, Palaearctic, African, Oriental and Australian. This is based on how the animals are believed to have evolved from common ancestors 200 million years ago, when there was a single landmass on Earth, Pangea. Most of the regions are made up of a single continent, such as Africa and Australia. The Palearctic and Oriental regions are separated mainly by the Himalayas, which act as a barrier to the movements of land animals.

Each region has its own characteristic collection of mammals, well-adapted to the local climate and vegetation. But where there are similar habitats within regions, such as the rain forests and grasslands of South America, Africa and Asia, the same types of mammals – monkeys, big cats and bats, for example – have evolved. Just how unique the mammals of a region are is related to the length of time that part of the world has been separated from the rest. The Australian region became isolated some 70 million years ago, longer than any other and before placental mammals had reached it, and its native mammals are all marsupials. North America, on the other hand, remained joined to Asia by a land bridge at the Bering Strait. Thus native American mammals are similar to those found in Eurasia.

Moose · Red fox · Caribou · Prairie dog · Racoon · NEARCTIC · Bison · Brown bear · Opossum · Vampire bat · Anteater · NEOTROPICAL · Vicuna · Guinea pig · Jaguar · Capybara

Movement

Among mammals, every method of locomotion is represented. Bats are specially adapted to flying, having front limbs with elongated fingers between which are stretched sheets of skin to form wings. Dolphins, porpoises and whales, along with dugongs and manatees, are adapted to life in water. They have a streamlined body and front legs modified into paddles that they use with great efficiency to swim and dive. Most carnivores, such as cheetahs, can walk and run fast. Tree-living species, in particular monkeys and apes, can swing from branch to branch, and some can walk on two legs. Flying squirrels and colugos have skin stretched between front and hind limbs that allows them to glide through the air.

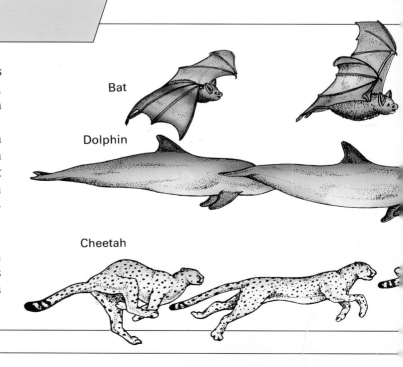

Bat · Dolphin · Cheetah

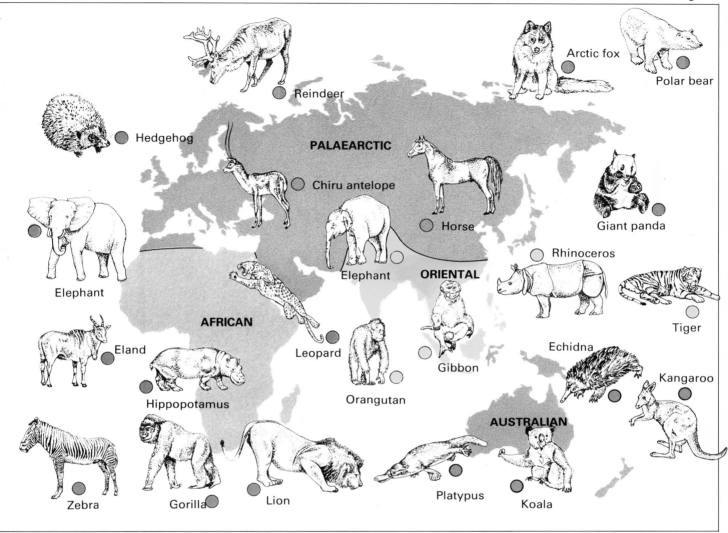

Reindeer

Arctic fox

Polar bear

Hedgehog

PALAEARCTIC

Chiru antelope

Horse

Giant panda

Elephant

Rhinoceros

Elephant

ORIENTAL

Tiger

AFRICAN

Leopard

Echidna

Kangaroo

Eland

Gibbon

Hippopotamus

Orangutan

AUSTRALIAN

Zebra

Gorilla

Lion

Platypus

Koala

○ Animals common to Nearctic and Palaearctic regions

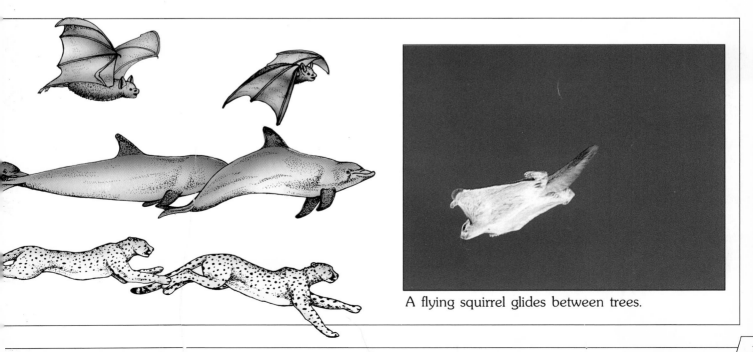

A flying squirrel glides between trees.

POUCHED AND EGG-LAYING

Monotremes: includes only the platypus of Australia and the spiny anteaters of Australia and New Guinea.
Marsupials: about 266 species. Small tree-living opossums (83 species) live in South America. Koalas, kangaroos, numbats, wombats, phalangers, bandicoots and native cats (183) live in the Australian region.

Apart from laying eggs, monotremes differ from other mammals in several ways. They have a lower, more variable body temperature, and the milk glands are modified sweat glands without a true teat. Their skeletons have some reptilian features, and they do not have separate body openings for excretion and reproduction. Marsupials are generally more like the placental mammals, but their mode of reproduction sets them apart. Although giving birth to young at an early stage of development restricts their lifestyle, they do show a wide variety of adaptations and feed on many different types of food. Marsupials include opossums, koalas and kangaroos.

Newborn

The platypus and the spiny anteater lay small leathery-shelled eggs rather like those of reptiles. The platypus lives in a burrow and lays its eggs in a nest chamber. The spiny anteater develops a pouch during the breeding season, and this provides a temporary home for the eggs and newly hatched young.

With marsupials, the baby remains in the mother's womb for a relatively short time. When it is born its organs are all well formed but few are really working. The baby crawls unaided to one of the mother's teats and seizes it in its mouth. The teat swells, and for a while the baby becomes a fixture into which the mother pumps milk. The baby grows rapidly. In many species a pouch encloses the teats for the young, but in some the teats just lie within a hollow in the abdomen. A newborn marsupial may bear little resemblance to the adult. A baby kangaroo is a thumb-sized creature with larger front limbs than back ones, still blind but with a sense of smell to guide it to the pouch. Once it has grown large it may start to leave the pouch for short periods. A new baby may be born when the previous young is becoming independent but still taking milk from the mother.

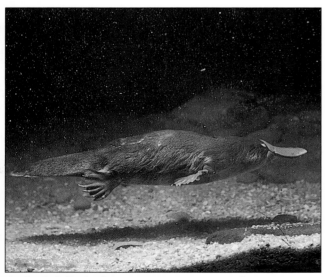

A duck-billed platypus swimming under water

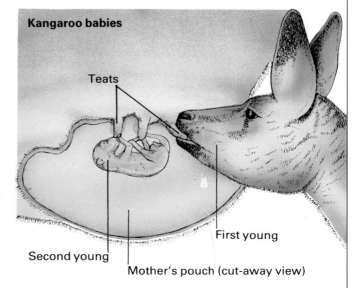

Kangaroo babies

Teats

First young

Second young

Mother's pouch (cut-away view)

Feeding

Koalas feed only on eucalyptus leaves.

A spiny anteater probes the ground for ants.

The familiar kangaroos and wallabies graze grasses or browse on the leaves of shrubs and young trees. Wombats feed on grasses, including the roots, with their constantly growing teeth. Koalas feed in trees on a specialized diet of eucalyptus leaves. Other specialist feeders include the tiny honey opossum, which has a brush-like tongue for lapping up the nectar of flowers. Meat-eaters include the native 'cats' and also a number of insect-eating marsupial 'mice.' The numbat feeds almost exclusively on termites.

All the monotremes (platypus and spiny anteaters) are toothless. The platypus swims well and catches many kinds of small animals with its beak. The spiny anteater can dig well, and licks up ants with its long tongue.

Evolution

Furry warm-blooded creatures resembling present-day mammals first evolved from reptiles during the Age of the Dinosaurs. The egg-layers probably had different ancestors than the other mammals. Some 100 million years ago, before the dinosaurs died out, the first relatives of our marsupial and placental mammals were living, but in a world where the continents were joined more closely than now. Marsupials were able to move from their first home in South America to Australia via Antarctica. Then the continents broke up, leaving most of the marsupials isolated in Australia, with only a few – the opossums – in South America. Evolution has followed a similar path in two, now very separate parts of the world.

Placental

Wolf

California mole

Marsupial

Tasmanian tiger

Marsupial mole

INSECT-EATERS

Major types: The order Insectivora includes moles (47 species), hedgehogs (15) and shrews (over 200). The bats, order Chiroptera, are the second most numerous mammal order, with over 900 species, most adapted to eating insects. Other insect-eaters include pangolins (7), South American anteaters (4) and armadillos (20).

The very first mammals to evolve were insect-eaters. Present-day shrews look similar to some of these early mammals and, like them, have small sharp teeth in their jaws to catch and chop insects and other small animals. Insect-eating remains a very successful way of life and shrews and their relatives are found almost worldwide. Insect-eating bats are another ancient group. They developed the ability to fly 50 million years ago and have been successfully eating the huge supply of flying insects ever since. Ants and termites are another large food source, and unrelated animals of many groups, including anteaters and armadillos, rely on them as their staple diet.

Feeding

Mammals with small bodies lose heat fast. Tiny hunters like shrews feed voraciously to obtain the energy to make up for this heat loss. They eat about their own body weight daily, sometimes even more. They constantly scurry through the undergrowth and leaf litter, pouncing on beetles, centipedes and spiders. Hedgehogs also feed on a variety of insects and slugs, but being larger can take life more slowly. Moles move through their network of underground tunnels, picking up worms and other juicy morsels. For pangolins, aardvarks and other anteaters food comes in very tiny packets. Large claws to break into nests, and a long sticky tongue to lick up large numbers very quickly, are more important than biting, and these animals have small simple teeth or none. Insect-eating bats have sharp teeth to seize and bite their food. Many use their wings to help gather their prey in flight. Some pick prey from leaves, others swoop over water to hunt.

A long-eared bat hunting a moth

Worms are a favorite food of European moles.

Active period

Shrews need so much food that they are active most of the day, but alternate periods of activity with short periods of rest. Bats, although they have a tiny body and a large surface, are not constantly active. They emerge at night to feed on nocturnal insects. During the day they hang at rest upside down and allow their body temperature to drop, so conserving energy until the night's activity.

Hundreds of bats emerging at sunset

Senses

Underground, moles have little use for eyes but their senses of hearing and smell are good. Their sense of touch is clearly important too, as can be seen from the large whiskers they have. Shrews have poor eyesight. In bats, too, eyesight is not very important. Insect-eating bats have such acute hearing that they are able to navigate and chase prey by listening to echoes of their own high-pitched voices.

A shrew sniffs the air for possible danger.

Hibernation

In the tropics there are usually insects available for most of the year, but in temperate regions there may be plenty in summer but few in winter. Shrews stay active all year but in winter have a hard time and many die. Hedgehogs solve the problem by hibernating. They find an undisturbed frost-free place and settle down to sleep, allowing the body temperature to drop very low. They stay barely alive — their hearts beat slowly and they scarcely breathe. Sometimes they wake and move from their nests, but in winter they are inactive, saving energy by not trying to stay 'warm-blooded.' Bats also hibernate during the coldest months.

A European hedgehog hibernating in a nest of leaves

RODENTS AND RABBITS

Within the order Rodentia there are 3 main groups:
Squirrel group, with kangaroo rats, marmots and beavers (377 species). Porcupine group, with African mole-rats and, from South America, guinea pigs, chinchillas (188). Mouse group, with rats, hamsters and jerboas (over 1,137). The order Lagomorpha includes rabbits, hares and pikas (58 species).

Rodents, a group that includes mice, rats and rabbits, are extremely successful mammals, found in nearly all habitats except the sea. Most live on the ground, although there are many – such as squirrels – that are good at climbing or living in trees. Others, like beavers and some voles, live in and around fresh water. Many use burrows for shelters and homes, but mole-rats and other species are adapted to a life burrowing underground and almost never come to the surface. The secrets of their success include their feeding methods and their ability to reproduce fast. Hares, rabbits and the similar pikas share some of the same adaptations but are not so varied.

Teeth and jaws

Rodents have a pair of large incisor teeth at the top and bottom of the front of the mouth. These grow continuously, and are used for gnawing into tough plant food, a process that wears the teeth down as fast as they grow. The enamel on the front of the incisors is hardest, so the teeth wear into a chisel shape. Along the side of the jaws are flattened chewing teeth. Rabbits have two pairs of chisel-shaped incisor teeth. They make good use of food by passing it through the gut twice, eating the feces produced the first time.

A porcupine shows its long front incisors.

Breeding

Many rodents produce great numbers of offspring. This is not so much because their litters are large – while some species produce as many as 17 young at a time, a more typical number is 4 – but because the young themselves become able to breed at an early age. In species such as mice, pregnancy lasts just a few weeks and those less than a year old may start to produce litters. In favorable conditions populations build up fast. Rabbits, too, breed fast. With no deaths, the offspring of a single pair could reach 33 million in 3 years.

House mice produce litters several times a year.

Homes

Rodents make their homes in a variety of places. Many climbing species rest in tree holes. Others make a ball nest from sticks, as do some squirrels, or from grasses or bark, as do harvest mice and dormice. Most rodent homes are not elaborate, but wood rats and stick-nest rats build large mounds of twigs to serve as weatherproof houses. These may have several compartments, including a place to store food and a latrine. The most elaborate aboveground structures are made by beavers, which make dams of sticks and mud to control water levels around the 'lodge' containing the family. Many rodents seek refuge down burrows. Some construct complex systems of tunnels with escape holes, nest chambers, storage places and latrines. Prairie dogs build a raised lip of soil around the entrance to keep out floodwater. The longest tunnels are those of mole-rats – more than 400m (440yd) long. The homes of rabbits are similar but less varied.

A beaver's dam and lodge in Alaska

Squirrels sometimes nest in holes in trees.

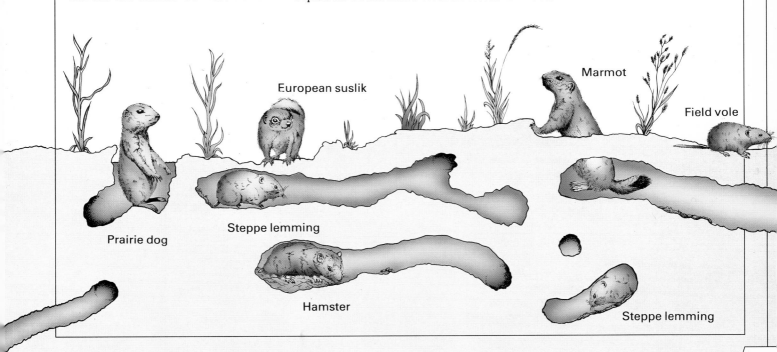

European suslik

Marmot

Field vole

Prairie dog

Steppe lemming

Hamster

Steppe lemming

WHALES AND PORPOISES

There are 2 major types:
Toothed whales (66 species), including river dolphins, beaked whales, dolphins and porpoises.
Whalebone (baleen) whales (10 species), including gray whale, rorquals and right whales.
Biggest species: Blue whale – more than 30m (100ft) long and weighing 140 tons.

The whale family comprises mammals completely adapted to life in water. The majority of the 80 or so species live in the open seas, and of these, many inhabit warm tropical waters, while others spend much of their lives in the cool polar seas. All are mammals that during evolution returned to the sea, where animal life began. They still have a fish-like appearance. Among them are the biggest animals ever to have lived on Earth, with the Blue whale at 140 tons. Whales have no hind limbs or external ears. Their forelimbs take the form of paddles, and they have a tail with flukes. Beneath the skin is a layer of blubber, or fat, which helps to conserve body heat in the water.

Breathing

Whales can stay under water for an hour or more. Yet they breathe air with their lungs and must surface to replace the oxygen their bodies need. They store oxygen in their muscles and on a dive use this and the oxygen in their lungs to stay alive. As they surface, they open the blowhole on top of their head and blow out the used air. Then they take one or more deep breaths. Underwater, the blowhole is closed by a valve and the windpipe is sealed off from the throat to prevent water entering the lungs when the animal feeds.

A fin whale blows water out of its blowhole.

Birth

Most whales do not reach maturity for many years. Pregnancy lasts from 8 months, for small dolphins, to 16 months or more for the big whales such as the blue, fin and sperm whales. Mostly only one offspring is produced. The baby is born under water tail-first. Immediately it surfaces, or its mother nudges its head out of the water, to take its first breath. The baby suckles milk from nipples hidden in folds on the mother's underside. Care of the young lasts weeks or months and is often carried out by all the females in a group.

A mother dolphin and her offspring

Feeding

Whales are divided into two main groups by the different types of jaws and feeding methods.

Toothed whales have narrow lower jaws and, as adults, cone-shaped pointed teeth in the lower or both jaws. The teeth number from 2 to 120 depending on the species. In nar-whals, one of the two upper-jaw teeth is greatly enlarged to form a spirally twisted tusk 2m (6.5ft) in length. Toothed whales feed mainly on fish and squid.

Baleen, or whalebone, whales lack teeth and the upper jaw is V-shaped and has up to 300 plates of horny material similar to matted hair or fingernails. These plates of baleen hang down from the jaw and act as strainers to sift out plankton, the tiny aquatic animals and plants. When baleen whales are not feeding, the plates are enclosed within the broad lower jaw.

A southern right whale feeding on plankton

A killer whale hunts in the Arctic Ocean.

Migration

There tend to be many separate populations of whales. Some inhabit just the Northern Hemisphere, others the Southern, and within each there are Pacific, Atlantic and Indian Ocean groups. Within each area, groups of whales may migrate many thousands of miles each year, following definite circuits. These sometimes take them close to the mainland or among the pack ice of polar regions. Most toothed whales migrate to keep up with the movements of the fish on which they feed. Among baleen whales, the males move north in summer and return to the tropics in winter for the breeding season.

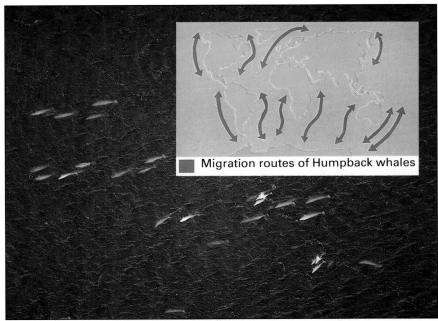

Migration routes of Humpback whales

A group of migrating beluga whales

<table>
<tr><td>

Major types: Odd-toed – includes tapirs and rhinos (9 species), horses, asses and zebras (7). Even-toed – includes pigs (9), hippos (2), camels (6), deer (37), cattle and antelope (121), giraffe (2). **Related to these:** seacows (4), elephants (2), hyraxes (11).

</td></tr>
</table>

One of the main common body features of non-fish vertebrates is the possession of two pairs of limbs, each bearing five digits (fingers or toes). In mammals these so-called pentadactyl limbs (from the Greek *penta* five, *dactyl* finger) have, during evolution, taken on such forms as the wings of bats and the flippers of seals or, as in dugongs and manatees, a pair has been lost. Hoofed mammals are generally medium-sized to large plant-eating animals in which finger and toe nails have become large, flat and greatly toughened as hooves. Hooves allow the animals to walk on their digits rather than on the soles of their feet as humans do, and allow good balance while running.

Hooves

There are two main groups of hoofed animals – odd-toed and even-toed. The odd-toed species have a variable number of digits on each foot but almost always three or one. For example, rhinoceroses have three, whereas horses have just one large central digit on each foot. Tapirs have four on the front feet and three on the hind feet. The weight of these animals is carried by the central digit or digits of each foot. Even-toed species have two or four digits on each foot. The more primitive kinds, such as pigs and peccaries, tend to have four digits per foot yet they rest their weight and walk on only two of these, usually the third and fourth. Camels, and the South American llama, guanaco and alpaca, have feet with two equal digits. Elephants have five digits per foot and these are spread out to support the animals' weight almost equally.

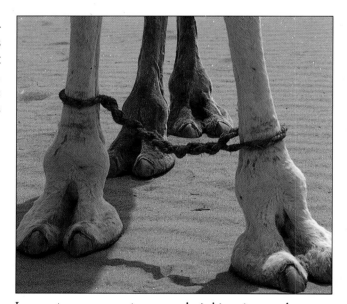

Large toes prevent a camel sinking in sand.

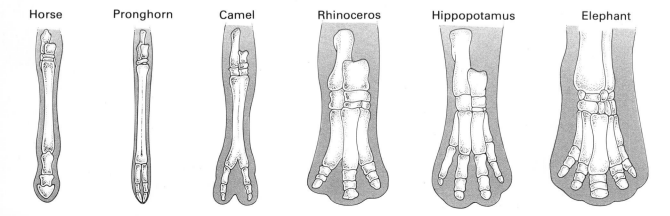

Horse   Pronghorn   Camel   Rhinoceros   Hippopotamus   Elephant

Digestion

Even-toed mammals are adapted to eating lots of plant material, ranging from roots to leaves and fruits. Pigs and their relatives, however, eat both plant and animal food. But they all have cheek teeth specialized for grinding vegetable material and a stomach that has several chambers for processing food in various ways. One group, which includes deer, giraffe, cattle and sheep, are said to chew the cud. Cud is food that is first stored in the stomach then returned to the mouth for chewing thoroughly. These animals are called ruminants. Odd-toed mammals also have grinding cheek teeth but the stomach is simple in structure and none of them chews the cud.

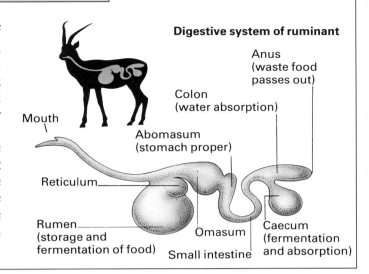

Digestive system of ruminant

Mouth

Reticulum

Rumen (storage and fermentation of food)

Abomasum (stomach proper)

Colon (water absorption)

Anus (waste food passes out)

Omasum

Small intestine

Caecum (fermentation and absorption)

Feeding

In the vast grasslands of Africa, South America and Eurasia there are large populations of various hoofed mammals living side by side. There is little competition for food between them because the different species do not have the same diet. In the Serengeti Plains of Africa, for example, zebras and rhinoceroses eat the short grass. Elands feed on the leaves of shrubs and young trees. Elephants use their long flexible trunk to strip leaves and bark from the upper branches of trees. Giraffes, with their long neck, can stretch even higher, above all the other plant-eaters, and reach leaves at the very top of tall trees.

Giraffe

Cape buffalo

Cape eland

Impala

Elephant

Gerenuk

Zebra

Wildebeest

White rhinoceros

Family life

Many hoofed mammals feed, sleep and travel across country in herds. Within these herds are several family groups. Elephants occasionally collect in the hundreds but usually move in herds of about 40 in which each member is related to all the others. The small herds consist of mothers and their young, sisters, cousins and aunts. Male elephants travel singly or in small all-male groups. Members of family herds communicate with one another by calls and scents. Living as a herd offers protection from enemies and allows the young to learn about their surroundings from elders.

A baby African elephant only three days old

Weapons

Where resources such as food or homes are limited, many animals of a species compete with one another. Some have evolved weapons to improve fighting ability in contests. Warthogs and elephants bear tusks, which are greatly enlarged teeth, and use them as battering rams. Various antelopes and their relatives, such as ibexes, duikers and waterbuck, have horns for jabbing and which they lock together and try and twist each other's heads down on to the ground. Similarly, most male deer grow branched antlers, which are bony outgrowths of the skull, and interlock these with those of their opponents as they try and push one another over. Antlers are shed each year while horns are permanent.

Male bighorn sheep fighting with their horns

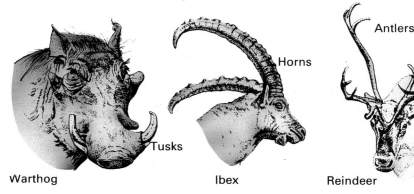

Warthog   Tusks   Horns   Ibex   Antlers   Reindeer

Mating

The reproductive behavior of hoofed mammals has been studied for centuries because the successful breeding of species such as sheep, goats, cattle and horses is the basis of domestication and animal farming. In the wild, females are 'in heat' — that is, ready to mate — at only certain times of the year, and in several species males and females live apart for many months then come together briefly for mating. Males of some species often compete with one another for the right to mate with females and have many 'wives.' Pregnancy generally lasts many months, and only one offspring is produced at a time. Domesticated animals, though, are bred to come in heat more than once a year and for multiple births.

American wild mustangs mating

Life in the water

Seacows, the dugong and manatees, like whales, are adapted to an aquatic way of life. They have a massive cigar-shaped body, paddle-like front legs, no hind legs, and have a flattened tail. To help conserve heat they have a thick layer of blubber. They spend all their lives in water, feeding, sleeping, mating and giving birth beneath the surface. They breathe through their nostrils on top of their rounded muzzle, surfacing frequently to replenish the air in their lungs.

Yet seacows are often grouped with hoofed mammals, with elephants and hyraxes as their closest relatives, because many have front legs with flattened horny nails. The dugong lives in warm waters off the coasts of South America, Southeast Asia and Australia. It is hairless and the male bears a pair of tusks. Manatees frequent estuaries of the Atlantic coasts of North America and Seacows are placid, sluggish animals that feed on plants such as eelgrass.

A heavy hippo can swim more easily than walk.

A manatee in a Florida river

MEAT-EATERS

Major types: Cat family (35 species), including lions, tigers, wild and domestic small cats. Dog family (35), including jackal, fennec, wolf, fox. Bears (7), raccoons and pandas (17), civet family (80) and weasel family (67). Seals, sea lions, walrus (33).

There are some 300 species of mammal that live on a substantial meat diet. They are known as carnivores. Some, such as lions and tigers, are predators, hunting live prey. Others, among them hyenas, are scavengers, taking the remains of other animals' kills. However, giant pandas feed almost exclusively on bamboo shoots, and aardwolves on carrion as well as insects. Closely related to true carnivores are seals, sea lions and the walrus, which are adapted to life in water. They feed mainly on fish and shellfish. Common to carnivores are strong jaws with large canine teeth and cheek teeth with cutting edges that slice against each other to tear and chew flesh.

Hunting

Most carnivores are solitary creatures and hunt for prey alone. A tiger, for example, stalks its prey then, when within striking distance, rushes at it. It knocks the animal down to the ground then grabs its throat in its powerful jaws. The prey, unable to breathe, dies quickly. Wolves and other members of the dog family hunt in packs of up to 30. They often surround an animal then close in for the kill. Weasels and stoats often chase their prey into underground burrows, and otters pounce on fish swimming in shallow water. Walruses do not hunt but rake up shellfish from the sea bed.

Wolves hunt together in packs.

Feeding

Big cats such as lions, cheetahs, panthers and tigers gorge on their kill in one meal and may not feed again for many days. Scavengers such as jackals eat whenever food is available but tend to look for a carcass each day. They have particularly strong cheek teeth that allow them to crack open bones to feed on the rich marrow inside. Carnivores such as bears and raccoons are omnivorous, having a mixed diet of animal and plant food. The brown bear will eat fish, carrion, plant food and, like the red fox, where it lives close to people will raid garbage cans for scraps of food.

A female tiger eating her prey

Scents and signals

Most carnivores except seals possess a pair of glands near their tail from which they can squirt a strong-smelling liquid. They use this scent to mark out their territory, attract a mate, or as a means of defense. To define their territories, wild cats and dogs spray scent on tree trunks and rocks around the boundaries. Female tigers, when ready to mate, use their scent to attract males, who then compete with one another for the female's favor. Skunks, when threatened, squirt their foul-smelling scent. They can squirt as far as 3m (10ft) and the scent is so bad that the attacker runs off. Civets produce a sweet-smelling scent, musk, that is used for perfumes.

A lynx marking its territory with scent

Breeding

A female cat or dog often mates with many males, a female otter or badger with just one. Among weasels, stoats and polecats, the females are often smaller than the males and become ready to mate at only one, regular time of the year. After mating, the fertilized egg does not immediately become attached to the wall of the mother's womb and grow. This is delayed so that the young will be born at a time of year when food is more likely to be plentiful. At mating time among seals, males and pregnant females haul themselves out on land. The much larger males fight fiercely for the females. Mating takes place a few days after pupping.

Male walruses will fight for mates.

MONKEYS AND APES

Major types: Most primitive types – tree shrews (18 species), lemurs (15), indri and sifakas (4), lorises, pottos, bush babies (10), tarsiers (3). New World monkeys (41) – tamarins, marmosets, spider monkeys. Old World monkeys (82) – langurs, baboons, colobuses. Apes (14) – orang-utan, chimpanzee, gorilla.

The first mammals to evolve were insect-eating, ground-living animals. One group of these gradually became adapted to living in trees. From these arose monkeys and apes and their relatives, which include small tree shrews and tarsiers, but also humans. They are often called primates, from the Latin *primus* meaning first or of the highest rank, because these mammals are the most highly developed of all animals. They have a large complex brain and keen senses of touch, hearing and vision. The eyes are set on the front of the head to give stereoscopic vision. The skeleton is unspecialized, with all limbs having five digits. Primates have adapted to many different forest habitats.

Movement

All primates show adaptations to living in trees. Stereoscopic vision is needed to judge distances accurately, as when leaping from tree to tree. Most New World monkeys have a prehensile tail, one that can grasp a branch to help cling to a tree. Most primates have hands and feet that can grasp objects well. They use them not only for movement but also to take fruit, leaves and insect grubs, which form the diet of most species. Indri and sifakas have longer legs than arms. They cling to trees in an upright position and, like lemurs, move on the ground by hopping. Gibbons have longer arms than legs and use them to swing between branches. Chimpanzees have evolved an upright stance and they can walk on two legs. Such adaptations, however, have restricted the range of non-human primates to tropical and subtropical forests and tree and grass areas.

Lemur

Tarsier

Gibbon

Chimpanzee

Diana monkey

Social life

The higher primates are mostly sociable animals living in family groups within feeding territories. They travel together across country or through the trees, usually for protection, with the females and their babies in the center of the group. Among species such as baboons and chimps, the young learn, mostly through play, to respect their elders and to know their place.

Grooming plays an important part in maintaining the status system within the group.

Chimpanzees with baby

Mammals chart

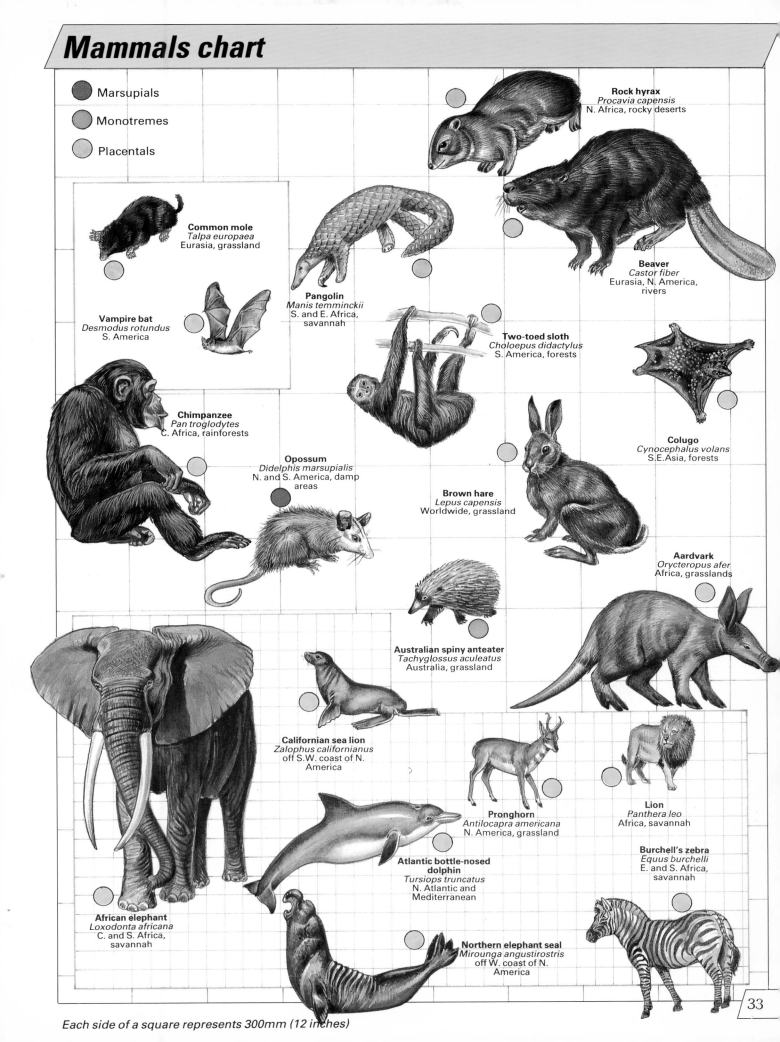

Marsupials

Monotremes

Placentals

Common mole
Talpa europaea
Eurasia, grassland

Vampire bat
Desmodus rotundus
S. America

Pangolin
Manis temminckii
S. and E. Africa,
savannah

Rock hyrax
Procavia capensis
N. Africa, rocky deserts

Beaver
Castor fiber
Eurasia, N. America,
rivers

Two-toed sloth
Choloepus didactylus
S. America, forests

Chimpanzee
Pan troglodytes
C. Africa, rainforests

Opossum
Didelphis marsupialis
N. and S. America, damp
areas

Brown hare
Lepus capensis
Worldwide, grassland

Colugo
Cynocephalus volans
S.E.Asia, forests

Aardvark
Orycteropus afer
Africa, grasslands

Australian spiny anteater
Tachyglossus aculeatus
Australia, grassland

Californian sea lion
Zalophus californianus
off S.W. coast of N.
America

Pronghorn
Antilocapra americana
N. America, grassland

Lion
Panthera leo
Africa, savannah

**Atlantic bottle-nosed
dolphin**
Tursiops truncatus
N. Atlantic and
Mediterranean

Burchell's zebra
Equus burchelli
E. and S. Africa,
savannah

African elephant
Loxodonta africana
C. and S. Africa,
savannah

Northern elephant seal
Mirounga angustirostris
off W. coast of N.
America

Each side of a square represents 300mm (12 inches)

CLASSIFICATION CHART

There are more than a million species of animal in the world. Biologists, scientists who study living creatures, have divided these up into several major groups based on the similarities between each kind and how they are believed to have evolved. Within the Animal Kingdom, the most important division is between those animals with a backbone, the vertebrates, and those without, the invertebrates. Vertebrates are in turn divided into 5 main categories, of which birds and mammals are considered to be the two most highly evolved. Within mammals a further division is made between egg-laying, pouched and placental mammals. This chart shows representatives of the main divisions.

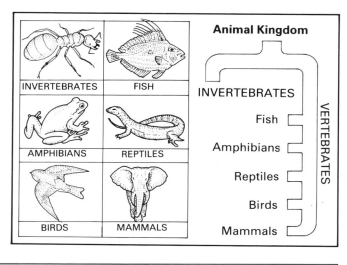

Animal Kingdom

INVERTEBRATES
- Fish
- Amphibians
- Reptiles
- Birds
- Mammals

VERTEBRATES

BIRDS

Kiwis | Ostrich | Rheas | Cassowaries and emu

Tinamous | Grebes | Divers and loons | Penguins

Albatrosses, shearwaters, petrels | Pelicans and relatives | Herons, storks, flamingoes | Screamers and ducks

Eagles, hawks, falcons | Game birds and hoatzin | Cranes and relatives | Waders, gulls, auks

Pigeons and sandgrouse | Parrots, macaws | Cuckoos and turacos | Owls

Frogmouths and nightjars | Swifts and hummingbirds | Mousebirds | Trogons

Kingfishers, hornbills | Woodpeckers, toucans | Perching birds

MAMMALS

Marsupials and placentals

PLACENTALS | MARSUPIALS

Monotremes

Insect-eaters | Colugos | Pouched mammals

Egg-laying mammals

Primates | Whales | Anteaters, sloths, armadillos

Pangolins | Rodents | Rabbits, hares, pikas

Meat-eaters | Seals, sea lions, walrus | Aardvark

Elephants | Hyraxes | Sea-cows

Odd-toed hoofed | Even-toed hoofed | Bats